**To Daniel French Thixton**

American Folktales for the primary grades,
full of action and humor, are about Amer-
ica's best known and most loved folklore
characters. Told in true tall-tale manner,
each story has a simple plot and colorful
illustrations. These delightful books, sure
to appeal to beginning readers everywhere,
are ideal for individualized or independent
reading in the classroom or library.

# THE STORY OF

# JOHNNY APPLESEED

## by LaVere Anderson

### illustrated by
### Kelly Oechsli

**GARRARD PUBLISHING COMPANY**
*CHAMPAIGN, ILLINOIS*

# THE STORY OF

# JOHNNY APPLESEED

Johnny was born in apple-picking time. The trees in his pa's orchard were red with apples under the September sun.

"Look at Johnny's legs!" his pa said. "With those long legs he'll soon be climbing the biggest trees in the orchard."

"I hope he won't use his long legs to run off where I can't find him," his ma said.

But Johnny did run off as soon as he was big enough.

Sometimes he ran one way, to the river. Sometimes he ran the other way, to the woods. His ma could never find him.

He learned to swim in the river. In the woods he learned how little wild animals lived. They became his friends, and he talked to them.

He could chatter like a squirrel
and bark like a fox. He could
bleat like a baby deer and whistle
like a woodchuck. All the animals
came when he called them.

Johnny talked to the birds too.

He could coo like a dove. He could squawk like a crow and hoot like an owl. Songbirds sat on his shoulders and sang to him. Johnny sang right back.

Johnny grew tall and strong. One day his pa told him, "You are too big to run off anymore. You must help me in the orchard."

Johnny worked hard in the orchard. He learned to plant apple seeds in the rich soil. He learned to take care of the seedling trees. At apple-picking time he climbed the biggest trees. He picked the

highest fruit. His ma could always find him now. All she had to do was look in the orchard.

"You are the best help I have ever had," his pa told him. "You eat the most apples, too."

"I like apples. They are good food," Johnny said. "I like raw apples, baked apples, applesauce, apple butter, and apple pie."

His pa laughed. "Then I am glad I planted plenty of apple trees."

"Everybody should plant apple trees," Johnny said. "When I grow up I am going to plant MILLIONS of them!"

"You will need a lot of ground for millions of trees. You won't find that much extra ground around here," his pa said.

Now, Johnny had been born in Leominster, Massachusetts, in 1774. Massachusetts was a well-settled state with many towns and farms, but Johnny had heard about unsettled land in the West. It was called the Ohio Valley.

It was wild country, but the soil was rich. People from eastern states were moving there.

"I'll go to the Ohio Valley," Johnny told his pa. "There is

plenty of land to be had for the asking. The new settlers will need apple trees."

"How will you find your way?" his pa asked.

"I'll follow the rivers. Rivers go everywhere."

Johnny grew taller and stronger. His legs grew longer. He thought more and more about the Ohio Valley.

One day he told his pa and ma, "I am a grown man now, and the house is crowded. It is time for me to go west." The house was crowded, all right. Johnny had ten young brothers and sisters.

Johnny's pa and ma were sad to see him go. He took with him a leather sack, packed with food and some apple seeds, a cooking pan, a flint to start campfires, his axe, and his knife.

"I won't need a gun," he said. "I would never kill an animal. Animals are my friends."

He followed the rivers. His long legs could cover the miles quickly.

Sometimes he stopped for a while and found a job. He helped farmers plant corn and chop wood.

"You are good help," they told him. "Stay here and live with us."

Johnny always shook his head. "Thank you, but I am going to the Ohio Valley. I want to plant apple orchards there."

The farmers laughed at that. They said, "The settlers in that wilderness will be busy building cabins and planting crops. They will have no time to take care of orchards."

"But they will like the apples," Johnny said. "Apples are the king of fruit, and fine food."

So away Johnny went, following the rivers.

At last Johnny came to Pennsylvania. There were many apple orchards in that state, and many cider mills. The millers squeezed the sweet juice from the apples. They did not need the apple seeds that were left. So they

let Johnny fill his leather sack to
the top with the biggest, fattest
seeds.

They laughed when he said he
was going to plant his seeds in
the Ohio Valley.

They said to him, "That is wild country. Deer will eat your young shoots. Bears will tramp down your seedling trees. You will never grow apples. Stay here with us."

Johnny thanked them, but he would not stay. Away he went, following the rivers.

With so many apple seeds in his sack, there was no room for his cooking pan. He could not throw the pan away. He needed it to cook his cornmeal mush.

"It will make a good hat," he thought, "and keep the rain off." So he put the pan on his head.

Soon he passed the last mill and the last farm. Now only forests lay between him and the Ohio Valley.

On and on he tramped. Winter came, and the forest was dark and cold. Snow began to fall. Soon it was so deep that it reached Johnny's knees. He could not make his way through such deep snow.

"I could freeze or starve to death," Johnny thought. "I had better do something."

He tore pieces of cloth off the bottom of his coat. He wrapped the pieces around his bare feet and legs.

"Now I have shoes and stockings," he said, "but what I need most are snowshoes."

He looked around the forest.
He saw a beech tree with long,
light branches and many twigs.

"There are my snowshoes!"
Johnny said.

He found dry wood and built
a campfire. He cut off some of the

thinnest beech branches and warmed them over his fire until they were soft. By bending and weaving the branches, he shaped them into snowshoes.

He tied the shoes to his feet with pieces of moosewood bark.

"This is the best pair of snowshoes in the forest!" Johnny laughed.

Then he tramped on. After many days he came to the Ohio Valley. He found some settlers and stayed with them until spring.

Oh, it was beautiful in the Ohio wilderness that spring when Johnny first came!

Everywhere he looked he saw bright birds and little friendly forest animals. The air was sweet with the smell of wild blossoms. Fish jumped in the rivers.

Johnny lost no time in planting

an orchard. He found an open
space beside a river. With a
pointed stick he poked holes in
the rich earth. Into each hole he
dropped an apple seed.

Then with his axe he chopped down some bushes. He built a bush fence around the new little orchard to protect it from animal feet.

When the settlers saw what he was doing, they laughed.

They said, "Don't you know that weeds will soon kill those seedlings? That fence won't last long either."

"I will come back to pull the weeds and mend the fence," Johnny said.

"It takes years for an apple tree to bear fruit. Are you coming back for years?"

"Only until there are seedling trees," Johnny said. "Then the new settlers can replant the trees in orchards near their cabins. You can replant some of them at your cabins too."

"We have no money to pay for trees," they said. "The new settlers will be as poor as we are. You won't be able to sell your seedlings."

Johnny looked surprised. "I do not mean to sell them. I will give them to all who want apple trees."

Now it was the settlers' turn to look surprised.

"What a strange man!" they thought. "He means to plant apple trees in the wilderness and then *give* them away."

Johnny planted many seeds. He found an old boat that nobody wanted. He used it to carry his seeds up and down the river.

One warm summer day Johnny heard a wolf howling. "OW-OOO. OW-OOO."

"He is in trouble!" Johnny exclaimed.

He rowed to shore and ran up the forest path. Rabbits and squirrels stopped their play to

watch him. Field mice came from the grass. A baby snake left its sunny log to watch. They were not afraid of Johnny.

Soon Johnny saw the wolf lying across the path. Oh, what a great fierce beast! Johnny ran straight to him.

"Poor fellow," he cried, "your foot is caught in a trap."

He pulled the jaws of the steel trap apart. The wolf was free, but his foot was badly hurt. He looked up at Johnny for help. Johnny got water from the river and bathed the foot.

"Don't be afraid, Wolf," Johnny said. "I'll stay with you until you can walk again."

After three days Wolf could walk. He was so happy he wagged his bushy tail.

Johnny bathed in the river and dried himself with bunches of grass.

He put on his raggedy clothes. He combed his long hair with his fingers and set his cooking pan on his head.

"Now I must leave you, Wolf," he said. "I have apple trees to plant. In time there will be blossoms for the wild bees. Some day there will be an apple for the traveler, an apple for the deer. There will be an apple for you too, Wolf, and apples for all the little children."

Johnny got into his boat and started to row away.

THUMP.

Johnny turned around and looked.

There sat Wolf in the back of the boat!

"Jumped in, did you?" Johnny said. "All right, you can come along."

Soon Johnny rowed to shore and went into a clearing. He poked holes in the ground. He dropped seeds.

Wolf watched. Then he began to scratch the ground with his sharp claws. Whish! Whish! Whish! How the dirt flew! In no time at all Wolf had dug a long row of holes.

"You are better than a pointed stick," Johnny said. He dropped a seed into each of Wolf's holes.

Johnny and Wolf planted many orchards together. They did not part until Johnny had to go back to the cider mill for more apple seeds.

Johnny returned with two big bags of seeds to plant.

As the years passed, he made friends with the Indians in the forest. He visited their camps and nursed their sick.

"Stay with us," they said. "Be our brother."

He made friends with the white settlers too. He helped them build cabins and plow fields.

"He spends his life helping others," they said. "He will take no pay except a little cornmeal."

He gave his seedling trees to all who wanted an apple orchard, and now everybody wanted one. He asked nothing for the trees, but sometimes settlers paid him with warm clothes or a few pennies.

Johnny gave the clothes to people he thought needed them more than he did.

He spent the pennies on presents for the settlers' children. Johnny liked children. In his sack there was always a pink hair ribbon for a little girl and a tin whistle for a boy.

Nobody laughed at Johnny anymore. He was welcome in every cabin. People called him Johnny

Appleseed, for nobody knew that his real name was John Chapman. He almost forgot it himself.

"Welcome, Johnny Appleseed!" they cried when he came to a cabin. "Have supper with us. Spend the night with us."

After supper Johnny always took a Bible from his sack.

"Do you want to hear some news right from heaven?" he asked.

Then by the firelight, he read to them.

Still, they thought him a strange man because he had no house with roof and door. His

home was the forest. His bed was
the ground, and his blanket was
the sky. He lived mostly on nuts
and berries, and he went barefoot
all year long.

They told each other wonderful
stories about his strange ways.
Some of the stories were true.
Some were only partly true.
Perhaps some were not true at all.
But people loved to tell them,
because they loved Johnny.

"Once Johnny lay sick and
helpless for a week in the woods,"
they said. "When he was found,
there were all sorts of animal

tracks around him. Dangerous animals had been there—panther and bear and wolf—but there wasn't a mark of claw or tooth on Johnny!"

"One day Johnny climbed into
a big hollow log to get out of the
rain," they said. "Guess who else
was in that log. A great black
bear! Johnny just snuggled up to
that bear and had a nice warm
nap."

"Oh, Johnny and bears are friends," they said. "You know how fierce a mother bear is. Once in the deep woods, Johnny was seen playing with three cubs while the mother bear looked on."

"Johnny loves every living thing," they said. "When he makes a bed of pine branches for himself, he leaves a hole so the rattlesnakes can crawl under it to stay warm."

And everybody knew how Johnny had saved a tiny town in Ohio from Indian attack. When the people learned that Indians would attack at sunrise, they needed help.

Johnny came to help. In the black of night, he ran 30 miles through the wilderness to a fort to ask for soldiers.

When the Indians saw the soldiers arrive at dawn, they went back to their camp. There was no attack.

Johnny was glad. He did not want to see his friends, red and white, fight one another. He wanted them to love and help each other.

For 40 years Johnny planted apple trees in the Ohio Valley. He worked for the good of all mankind.

When he died, at 71, everybody
missed him.

At sunset, when clouds in the
sky turned pink as apple blossoms,
they looked up and said, "Johnny's
orchard is in bloom." When they

saw an old apple tree deep in the forest, far from any cabin, they said, "Johnny must have been this way."

And in Massachusetts, where he was born, the people built a stone monument in memory of Johnny Appleseed. On it are engraved the beautiful words:

HE PLANTED SEEDS
THAT OTHERS MIGHT ENJOY FRUIT.